Living LARGE

A Horse's Life

Sara Antill

PowerKiDS press
New York

Published in 2012 by The Rosen Publishing Group, Inc.
29 East 21st Street, New York, NY 10010

First Edition

Editor: Jennifer Way
Book Design: Greg Tucker

Photo Credits: Cover, pp. 4, 5, 6 (top, bottom), 7, 8, 9, 10, 11, 13, 14 (top, bottom), 15 (top, bottom), 16, 17, 18, 19, 20, 21, 22 Shutterstock.com; p. 12 Tom Robinson/Getty Images.

Library of Congress Cataloging-in-Publication Data

Antill, Sara.
  A horse's life / by Sara Antill. — 1st ed.
      p. cm. — (Living large)
  Includes index.
  ISBN 978-1-4488-4980-2 (library binding) — ISBN 978-1-4488-5108-9 (pbk.) —
  ISBN 978-1-4488-5109-6 (6-pack)
  1. Horses—Life cycles—Juvenile literature. I. Title. II. Series.
  SF302A58 2012
  636.1—dc22

2011000096

Manufactured in the United States of America

CPSIA Compliance Information: Batch #WS11PK: For Further Information contact Rosen Publishing, New York, New York at 1-800-237-9932

Contents

Meet the Horse

Have you ever spent time around a horse? You may have seen a horse on a farm, in a petting zoo, or running a race. Some families even own their own horses! These large animals have lived closely with people for thousands of years.

People use horses for racing, riding, and farmwork. You may even see horses carrying police on patrol in cities.

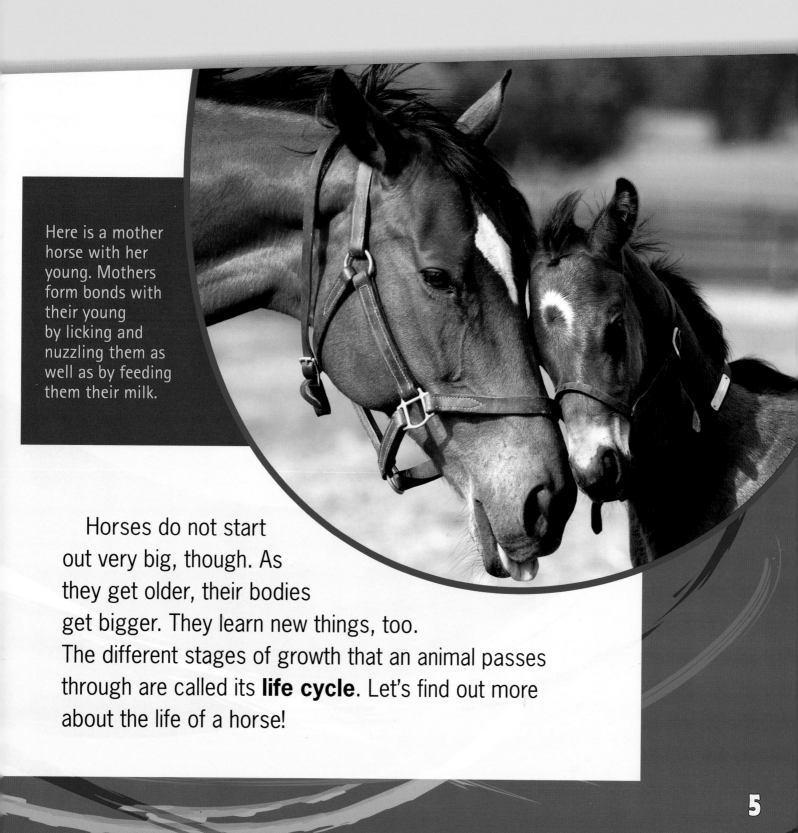

Here is a mother horse with her young. Mothers form bonds with their young by licking and nuzzling them as well as by feeding them their milk.

Horses do not start out very big, though. As they get older, their bodies get bigger. They learn new things, too. The different stages of growth that an animal passes through are called its **life cycle**. Let's find out more about the life of a horse!

How Many Hands?

There are around 400 different **breeds** of horses. Some horses, like Arabians, are fast. Most racehorses are Arabians. Other breeds, such as Clydesdales, are called draft horses. They are heavy and strong. These horses are often used to pull heavy carts or wagons.

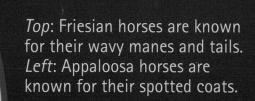

Top: Friesian horses are known for their wavy manes and tails. *Left*: Appaloosa horses are known for their spotted coats.

Arabian horses are one of the most popular horse breeds. This Arabian has a reddish brown coat. This color is known as bay.

Horses are measured using **hands**. One hand is equal to 4 inches (10 cm). The horses used for riding are generally between 14 and 17 hands tall and weigh between 840 and 1,300 pounds (380–600 kg). Draft horses are generally between 16 and 18 hands tall and weigh 1,500 to 2,200 pounds (700–1,000 kg).

Wild Horses

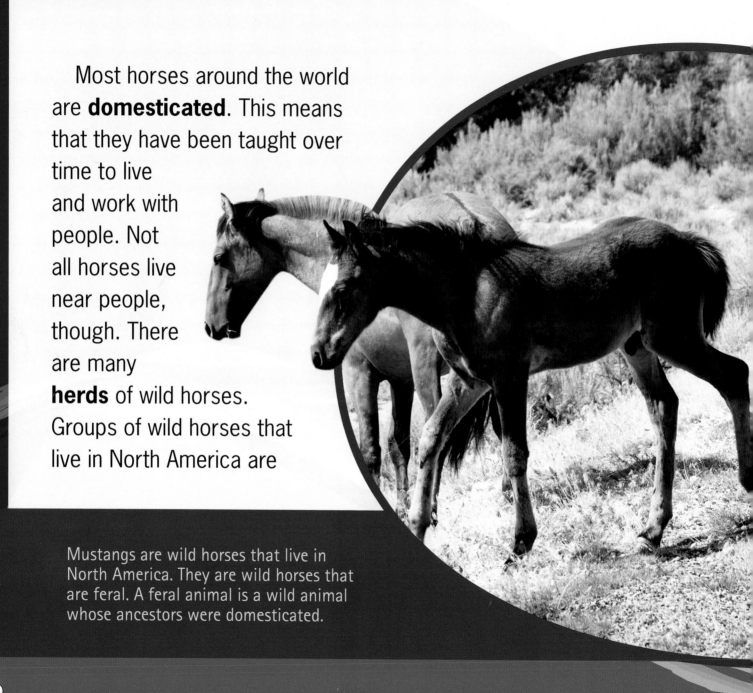

Most horses around the world are **domesticated**. This means that they have been taught over time to live and work with people. Not all horses live near people, though. There are many **herds** of wild horses. Groups of wild horses that live in North America are

Mustangs are wild horses that live in North America. They are wild horses that are feral. A feral animal is a wild animal whose ancestors were domesticated.

called mustangs. Wild horses live on grassy plains around the world.

Horses are **herbivores**. This means that they eat only plants. Horses eat mostly grasses. Domesticated horses also eat hay and grain. A horse that weighs 1,000 pounds (454 kg) can eat 15 to 24 pounds (7–11 kg) of food each day.

Wild horses live in groups, called herds.

Hooves and Teeth

Horses walk on **hooves**. A horse's hooves are made of the same material that a person's fingernails are made of. Sometimes a horse's owner will have the horse fitted for horseshoes. Metal horseshoes keep the horse's hooves safe. A horse's

Horseshoes keep a horse's hooves safe from cracking and other wear and tear.

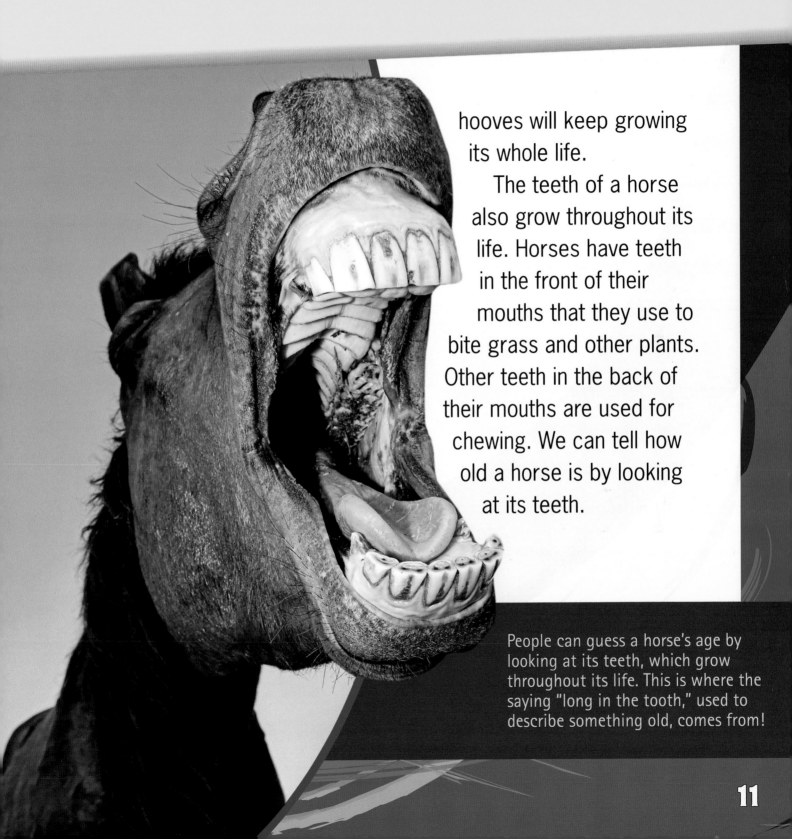

hooves will keep growing its whole life.

The teeth of a horse also grow throughout its life. Horses have teeth in the front of their mouths that they use to bite grass and other plants. Other teeth in the back of their mouths are used for chewing. We can tell how old a horse is by looking at its teeth.

People can guess a horse's age by looking at its teeth, which grow throughout its life. This is where the saying "long in the tooth," used to describe something old, comes from!

Strange Sleepers

Horses have very good eyesight. In fact, they have the largest eyes of any land **mammal**. Their eyes are on the sides of their heads. This means that they can see in many directions. Horses also have good hearing. In the wild, they use their sharp senses to stay safe from **predators**.

Horses can sleep while standing up. The sleep they get when lying down is a deeper sleep than standing sleep.

Another way that
horses in the wild
stay safe is sleeping
while standing up. They
do not sleep for many hours
at a time, as people do. In one
day, a horse takes several short
naps, each lasting about 15 minutes.

Life Cycle of a Horse

1 When a baby horse is born, it generally weighs around 50 to 80 pounds (23–36 kg). Baby horses can stand up and walk soon after they are born. For the first several months of its life, a baby horse will drink milk from its mother.

4 Wild horses are ready to **mate** at about two years old. Domesticated horses are generally not allowed to mate until they are around three years old. Mares give birth 11 months after they mate. Mares generally give birth to one baby at a time.

A young female horse is called a filly. A young male is called a colt. When a colt is two years old, it will leave its family group. Young horses grow quickly. By the time a horse is between four and six years old, it will be fully grown.

2

Adult male horses are called stallions. Adult females are called mares. By the time a domesticated horse is fully grown, it will know how to live and work around people.

3

15

Foals

When a young horse is born, it is called a **foal**. Foals can stand and run very soon after they are born. Foals cannot eat grass yet, though. Their legs are too long for their mouths to reach the ground! For the first five to seven months of their lives, foals live off milk from their mothers.

Foals stay close to their mothers for the first five to seven months of their lives.

Between the ages of one and two, young horses are called yearlings. When they are two years old, many domesticated horses will start to learn how to walk with a saddle and carry a rider.

Foals grow quickly. They can put on up to 3 pounds (1 kg) every day!

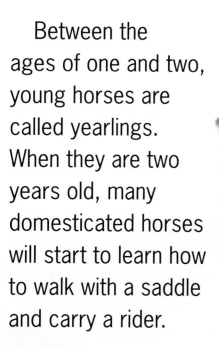

Growing Up

Horses live in groups, called herds. An adult male horse generally leads a herd. The other members of the herd are adult female horses and foals. There are generally between 3 and 20 horses in a herd.

Here is a colt. After a wild colt leaves its birth herd, it may form a herd with other colts. This is called a bachelor herd.

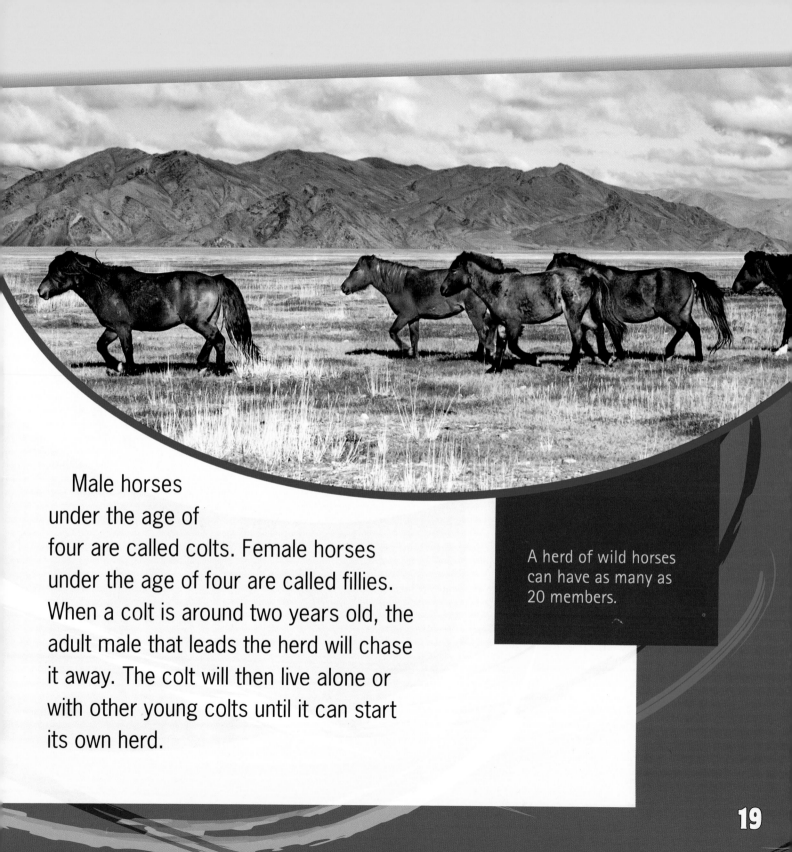

Male horses under the age of four are called colts. Female horses under the age of four are called fillies. When a colt is around two years old, the adult male that leads the herd will chase it away. The colt will then live alone or with other young colts until it can start its own herd.

A herd of wild horses can have as many as 20 members.

Stallions and Mares

Horses are thought to be adults at the age of four. Their bodies will keep growing until they are about six years old, though. Male horses older than four are called stallions. Females older than four are called mares. Most horses will live between 25 and 30 years.

Horses communicate with each other with sounds and body language.

Around the age of two, wild horses are ready to mate, or have babies of their own. Most domesticated horses do not mate until they are closer to three years old. Once a mare has mated, she will give birth to her foal after about 11 months.

Between the ages of two and four, domesticated horses are trained to wear saddles and carry people.

Our Special Friends

Horses are social animals. They talk to each other with sounds and movements of their tails. Many horses also have close bonds with people. For many years, people have depended on horses to do hard work. Almost all wild horses living today had relatives that once lived with humans.

Many people keep horses as pets.

Today, there is only one kind of wild horse that has never been domesticated. These horses, called Przewalski's horses, are **extinct** in the wild. There are only a few left in zoos. Many people are trying to help these horses survive, though, just as other horses have helped people survive for thousands of years.

Glossary

breeds (BREEDZ) Groups of animals that look alike and have the same relatives.

domesticated (duh-MES-tih-kayt-ed) Raised to live with people.

extinct (ik-STINGKT) No longer existing.

foal (FOHL) A baby horse.

hands (HANDZ) Measurements used for the height of horses. One hand is equal to 4 inches (10 cm), about the width of an adult human hand.

herbivores (ER-buh-vorz) Animals that eat only plants.

herds (HURDZ) Groups of the same kind of animals living together.

hooves (HOOVZ) The hard coverings on the feet of certain animals.

life cycle (LYF SY-kul) The different stages in an animal's life, from birth to death.

mammal (MA-mul) A warm-blooded animal that has a backbone and hair, breathes air, and feeds milk to its young.

mate (MAYT) To come together to make babies.

predators (PREH-duh-terz) Animals that kill other animals for food.

Index

B
bodies, 5, 20

G
grass(es), 9, 11, 16
growth, 5

H
hay, 9
herbivores, 9
herd(s), 8, 18–19
horseshoes, 10

L
life cycle, 5

M
mammal, 12
mustangs, 9

N
North America, 8

O
owner, 10

P
people, 4, 8, 13, 15, 22
plains, 9
plants, 9, 11
predators, 12

R
race, 4

S
stages, 5

T
teeth, 11

W
wagons, 6
wild, 12–13, 22

Z
zoo(s), 4, 22

Web Sites

Due to the changing nature of Internet links, PowerKids Press has developed an online list of Web sites related to the subject of this book. This site is updated regularly. Please use this link to access the list:
www.powerkidslinks.com/livl/horse/